A NOTE TO PARENTS

Reading Aloud with Your Child

Research shows that reading books aloud is the single most valuable support parents can provide in helping children learn to read.

- Be a ham! The more enthusiasm you display, the more your child will enjoy the book.
- Run your finger underneath the words as you read to signal that the print carries the story.
- Leave time for examining the illustrations more closely; encourage your child to find things in the pictures.
- Invite your youngster to join in whenever there's a repeated phrase in the text.
- Link up events in the book with similar events in your child's life.
- If your child asks a question, stop and answer it. The book can be a means to learning more about your child's thoughts.

Listening to Your Child Read Aloud

The support of your attention and praise is absolutely crucial to your child's continuing efforts to learn to read.

- If your child is learning to read and asks for a word, give it immediately so that the meaning of the story is not interrupted. DO NOT ask your child to sound out the word.
- On the other hand, if your child initiates the act of sounding out, don't intervene.
- If your child is reading along and makes what is called a miscue, listen for the sense of the miscue. If the word "road" is substituted for the word "street," for instance, no meaning is lost. Don't stop the reading for a correction.
- If the miscue makes no sense (for example, "horse" for "house"), ask your child to reread the sentence because you're not sure you understand what's just been read.
- Above all else, enjoy your child's growing command of print and make sure you give lots of praise. *You are your child's first teacher—and the most important one. Praise from you is critical for further risk-taking and learning.*

—Priscilla Lynch
Ph.D., New York University
Educational Consultant

Paintings by Ken Marschall
Front Cover, 3, 12-13, 16-17, 19, 21, 22-23, 40-41, 43 (Top), 46, 48

1: Private Collection 4: Emory Kristof © *National Geographic* Society 6: Emory Kristof © *National Geographic* Society, (Inset) Woods Hole Oceanographic Institution 8: The Father Browne S.J. Collection, (Inset) Don Lynch Collection 11: National Maritime Museum/Ken Marschall Collection 12: (Left and right insets) Ken Marschall Collection 13: (Left inset) Ken Marschall Collection, (Right inset) Private Collection 14: Ken Marschall Collection 24-25: *The Illustrated London News* 27: Brown Brothers 28: Private Collection 29: *The Illustrated London News* 30: Photo by Dann Blackwood/Woods Hole Oceanographic Institution 33: (Top left) Woods Hole Oceanographic Institution, (Top right) Emory Kristof © *National Geographic* Society, (Bottom) Emory Kristof © *National Geographic* Society 35: Emory Kristof © *National Geographic* Society 37: (Top left and right) Perry Thorsvik © *National Geographic* Society (Bottom) Photo by Martin Bowen 39: Woods Hole Oceanographic Institution 43: (Bottom left) Joseph Carvalho Collection, (Bottom right) Woods Hole Oceanographic Institution 44: All photos by Robert Ballard and Martin Bowen/Woods Hole Oceanographic Institution 45: Photo by Robert Ballard and Martin Bowen/Woods Hole Oceanographic Institution

Copyright © 1993 by Madison Press Limited.
All rights reserved. Published by Scholastic Inc.
CARTWHEEL BOOKS is a registered trademark of Scholastic Inc.
HELLO READER! is a registered trademark of Scholastic Inc.

Library of Congress Cataloging-in-Publication Data

Ballard, Robert D.

   Finding the Titanic / by Robert Ballard.

      p.   cm. — (Hello reader. Level 4)

   Summary: Describes the voyage of the Titanic, the accident that caused it to sink, and the rescue of those who survived.

   ISBN 0-590-47230-5

   1. Titanic (Steamship)—Juvenile literature. 2. Shipwrecks—North Atlantic Ocean—Juvenile literature. 3. Underwater exploration—North Atlantic Ocean—Juvenile literature. [1. Titanic (Steamship) 2. Shipwrecks.] I. Title. II. Series.
G530.T6B495 1993

909'.09634—dc20   93-19203
                                                    CIP
                                                    AC

23 22   8/9

Printed in the U.S.A.   23
First Scholastic printing, November 1993

Produced by
Madison Press Books
40 Madison Avenue
Toronto, Ontario
Canada M5R 2S1

FINDING THE
TITANIC

by Robert D. Ballard
with Nan Froman
Paintings by Ken Marschall

Hello Reader! – Level 4

Scholastic Inc. Cartwheel ·B·O·O·K·S·®

New York Toronto London Auckland Sydney

Produced by Madison Press Books

CHAPTER ONE
August 25, 1985

I went to the control center of our ship. "Have you seen anything yet?" I asked my team. I looked at the video screen. Nothing had appeared.

We were searching for the *Titanic* — the most famous of all shipwrecks. The *Titanic* was once the largest ship in the world. It had grand rooms. It seemed like a floating palace. Some people even said the ship was unsinkable.

But on its first voyage in April 1912, the *Titanic* hit an iceberg and sank. It was carrying over two thousand people. Many of them died when the ship went down.

I watch as we lower *Argo,* our underwater camera sled.

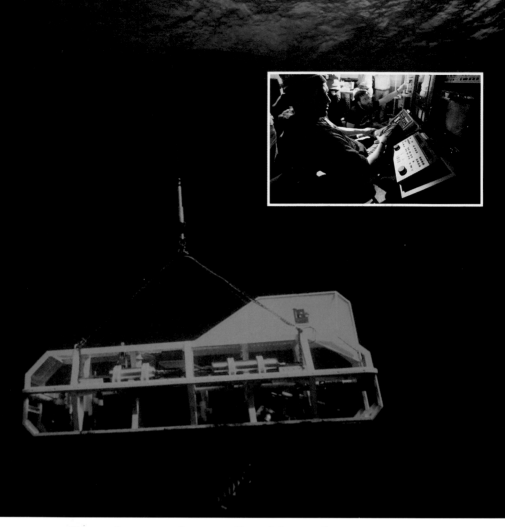

From the control center, I could see what *Argo* saw.

I had dreamed of finding the *Titanic* since I was a boy. No one had seen it in almost seventy-five years. It lay two and a half miles down on the bottom of the Atlantic Ocean. This is far deeper than any diver can go.

We built an underwater sled, *Argo*, to search for the ship. This sled took moving video pictures as it was pulled along just above the ocean floor. We watched these moving pictures on our ship's video screen.

We began our search where the *Titanic*'s lifeboats had been found by a rescue ship. For days we pulled *Argo* along above the ocean bottom. Nothing appeared on our video screen but mud. I wondered if the ship had been buried by an underwater mudslide.

I kept my eyes on the screen. But I thought about the people who survived the shipwreck. They told stories that will never be forgotten.

Ruth Becker

CHAPTER TWO
April 10, 1912

"It's so big!" cried twelve-year-old Ruth Becker. The huge black hull of the *Titanic* sat in the docks at Southampton, England.

The Becker family had been living in India. But now Ruth's brother was ill. Mrs. Becker decided to take her children back to America. So Mrs. Becker, Ruth, four-year-old Marion, and two-year-old Richard had sailed from India to England. Now they would board the *Titanic* for the trip to New York.

Ruth could hardly wait to get on the beautiful new ship. Yellow letters on the bow proudly spelled out the name: TITANIC. The *Titanic* was the largest ship afloat. It had nine decks and it was as tall as an eleven-story building. You could walk for miles along its decks and passageways.

The Beckers boarded the *Titanic,* and a steward helped them find their cabin.

"This is just like a hotel room!" Ruth said.

Before the ship set sail, Ruth decided to explore. She climbed up the Grand Staircase. Gold-plated light fixtures hung from the ceiling. Sunlight shone through a big glass dome overhead.

Ruth found the rooms of the wealthy first-class passengers. One of the doors was open. Ruth peeked inside. This room was bigger than her whole cabin. It was fancier, too.

Ruth stepped into an elevator near the Grand Staircase. She went down as far as it would go. She discovered a swimming pool and steam baths.

A second-class cabin like the one Ruth Becker had.

The hallways in the lower decks of the *Titanic* were crowded. Families carried large trunks and suitcases. Ruth heard many different languages. These were the third-class passengers. Many of them were hoping to make new lives for themselves in America.

A loud whistle sounded. Ruth hurried back to her cabin. It was noon — sailing

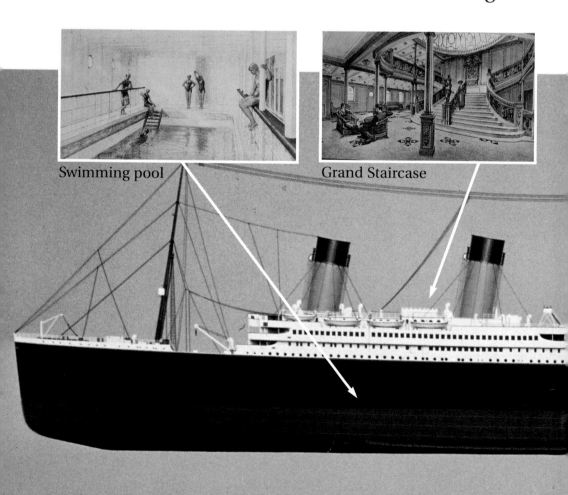

Swimming pool

Grand Staircase

time. She and her family went onto the boat deck.

Hundreds of passengers cheered as the *Titanic* pulled away from the dock. They waved to their friends on shore. There were even small boats waiting in the water. These boats were filled with people who wanted to see the biggest ship in the world set sail.

Second-class dining room   A second-class cabin

For the first few days of the voyage the weather was clear and the ocean was calm. The Beckers ate their meals in the second-class dining room. They sat at long tables with many other passengers.

On Sunday afternoon it became very cold. Ruth sat with her mother and some of the other passengers in the lounge.

"We're making good speed," one man said. "We might even arrive in New York early — if we don't run into ice."

"So I hear," said Mrs. Becker.

"I wouldn't mind seeing an iceberg, though," he continued. "I'm told they're quite a sight."

The *Titanic* at the dock.

CHAPTER THREE

April 15, 1912 — 12:30 A.M.

"Ruth, Ruth, wake up!"

Where am I? Ruth wondered. She rubbed her eyes. Then she remembered. She was on board the *Titanic*. But why did

her mother sound so frightened?

"Get out of bed and put coats on the children," her mother continued. "The ship has hit an iceberg! We're supposed to go up to the deck."

Now Ruth was wide awake. She got out of bed and quickly dressed Marion and Richard. The Beckers left their cabin. In their hurry, they forgot their life belts.

The family joined a group of passengers waiting to be led up to the boat deck. Some of them were fully dressed. Others, like Ruth and her mother, had coats over their nightclothes.

"It sounded just like the ship ran into gravel," one woman said.

Everyone wanted to know more about what had happened. Had the iceberg made a big hole? How serious was the damage? Was water flowing into the ship?

A crewman arrived and took the passengers to the lifeboats. "Women and children first!" people shouted.

Someone lifted Marion and Richard into lifeboat No. 11. "That's all for this boat," an officer said.

"Oh, please let me go with my children!" Mrs. Becker cried. A seaman helped her into the lifeboat. But Ruth was left behind!

"Ruth!" her mother screamed. "Get in another boat!"

Ruth walked over to the next boat. "May I get in?" she asked an officer. He lifted her into lifeboat No. 13. It was so crowded that Ruth had to stand up.

"Lower away!" the officer shouted. The boat dropped jerkily toward the sea. Ruth looked up at hundreds of passengers still on board the *Titanic*. There were not enough lifeboats for all of them.

Ruth's boat reached the water safely. But no one knew what to do or where to go. The passengers on board asked one of the crew to be their captain.

"Row toward those lights in the distance," he ordered. "They might be the lights of a ship that could pick us up."

Ruth looked back at the *Titanic*. Rockets went up from the ship sending bursts of stars into the sky. They were distress signals calling any nearby ships to come and help.

The bow of the *Titanic* was sinking. Ruth looked at the people still on board. They were trying to move back toward the stern. The ship's lights went out. Suddenly there was a loud noise like thunder. The *Titanic* broke apart. Ruth watched people leap into the sea.

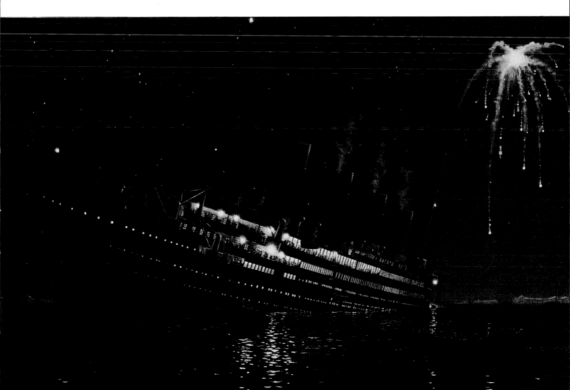

The bow disappeared under the water. For a minute the stern stood straight up in the

ocean. It looked like a huge whale. Then the *Titanic* dove beneath the waves.

CHAPTER FOUR
April 15, 1912 — 3:00 A.M.

"The sea will be covered with ships tomorrow," said a crewman in Ruth's boat. "They will race from all over to find us."

The lifeboats from the *Titanic* drifted on the calm, cold ocean. The survivors tried to keep the boats together by

calling out to one another in the dark.

Ruth heard a rocket. In the distance she spotted a faint green light. Could it be a rescue ship? Everyone in the boat who had a scrap of paper lit a match to it. They held these "torches" up high in the air. Maybe someone would see them.

The passengers at the oars rowed toward the lights. As they drew closer, they could see that the lights came from a large ship.

The ocean became rough. Ruth was drenched by the cold, splashing water.

Finally the lifeboat pulled alongside the rescue ship. Crewmen on board lowered a swing down to the boat. Ruth's hands were too numb to grasp the ropes. Someone had to tie her into the swing. The crew pulled her up the side of the ship. Its solid deck felt good beneath her feet.

Ruth went up to the ship's open deck. Most of the lifeboats had come in, but there was no sign of her family.

Then Ruth felt a tap on her shoulder. "Are you Ruth Becker?" a woman said. "Your mother has been looking for you!" She led Ruth to the second-class dining room.

Mrs. Becker, Marion, and Richard threw their arms around her. Ruth's eyes filled with tears of relief.

Some of the *Titanic*'s passengers prepare to board the rescue ship from their lifeboat.

The crew of the rescue ship, the *Carpathia*, searched the sea for several hours. But no more survivors were found.

Several days later, the *Carpathia* arrived in New York City harbor. Thousands of

people waited in pouring rain to greet the survivors. Ruth heard cries of joy from the people who had found their loved ones. But many others looked sad as they searched for family and friends who had drowned.

Titanic survivors arrive in New York City.

CHAPTER FIVE
August 31, 1985

Almost seventy-five years had passed since the *Titanic* sank. And now my team and I searched for the wreck. As each day went by, I wanted to find the lost ship more than ever.

Our time was running out. We hadn't seen a single sign of the wreck. We sometimes wondered if the *Titanic* really did lie on the ocean floor.

Late one night, Stu Harris pointed to the video screen. "There's something." The sleepy crew looked at the screen. They could see pictures of man-made objects.

Our search ship, the *Knorr.*

"Bingo!" Stu yelled. *Argo*'s cameras picked up a huge boiler on the ocean floor. Boilers burned coal to drive a ship's engines. This one had to belong to the *Titanic*!

Soon we saw pieces of railing and other wreckage. At last my dream was about to come true. The *Titanic* must lie nearby. Everyone was shaking hands and slapping one another on the back.

Someone noticed that it was 2 A.M., close to the time that the *Titanic* had sunk. We were excited, but we felt sad, too. We held a few moments of silence in memory of those who had sailed on the great ship so long ago.

Our first video run over the wreckage with *Argo* was risky. We weren't sure where the main part of the ship was. I was afraid that *Argo* might crash into it.

One of the *Titanic*'s boilers lying on the ocean floor.

This is how the huge boilers looked before they were placed in the ship.

I celebrate finding the *Titanic* with my crew.

All of a sudden, the huge side of the ship appeared. The *Titanic* was sitting upright on the ocean floor!

Over the next few days we made some important discoveries. The ship had broken in two sections. We saw large holes in the deck of the bow section where the funnels had once stood.

But at the end of our trip many mysteries still remained. What did the ship look like inside? Where was the hole made by the iceberg? And what lay scattered on the ocean floor around the wreck? Only another visit to the *Titanic* would tell us what we wanted to know.

Our underwater camera sled returns from photographing the *Titanic* more than 12,000 feet below the sea.

CHAPTER SIX
July 13, 1986

A year later we were ready to explore the *Titanic* from *Alvin,* our three-man submarine. I took off my shoes and climbed in.

We were squeezed inside *Alvin*'s tiny cabin. Soon we began our long fall to the ocean bottom. As we went down, it became colder and darker inside the little submarine.

When *Alvin* reached the bottom, I peered out my window. Where was the *Titanic?* We could only see a short distance in the darkness of the deep ocean.

The pilot turned *Alvin,* and we glided along the ocean floor. I stared out the window. The bottom looked very strange.

I climb inside our small submarine, *Alvin*.

Alvin is lowered into the water.

We work inside *Alvin* on our way to the ocean bottom.

It seemed to slope sharply upward. My heart beat faster.

Suddenly an enormous black wall of steel loomed in front of us. It was the *Titanic*!

The next day we explored the bow section of the ship. The bottom part of the bow was buried in mud. But I could see the large anchors still hanging in place.

We rose slowly up the ship's side. To my surprise, the glass in many of the portholes was not broken. I searched for the yellow letters spelling out the name TITANIC. But they were covered with rust.

Alvin began to move over the forward deck of the ship. Its wooden planks had been eaten away by millions of tiny sea worms.

We passed over the bridge of the ship. From here the captain and his officers had steered the *Titanic*.

The tip of the bow of the *Titanic*.

We headed toward the Grand Staircase. Its big glass dome was gone. This would be the perfect place for our small robot, *Jason Junior*, to go inside the ship. Then we could take close-up pictures.

The next morning we landed *Alvin* near the opening to the Grand Staircase. At last *Jason Junior*, or *JJ*, would see inside.

The bow section of the *Titanic* on the ocean floor.

JJ's pilot slowly guided our robot out of its little garage on the front of *Alvin*. *JJ* floated over the hole in the deck where the staircase had once been. The little robot went down into the ship and we lost sight of it. We watched the video screen inside our submarine to see what *JJ* was looking at.

A room appeared on the screen. "Look at that chandelier," *JJ*'s pilot exclaimed. It was one of the light fixtures which had lit Ruth Becker's way up the Grand Staircase. The metal part of the light was still bright and shiny.

We explored most of the great wreck over the next few days. *JJ* took a close-up look at the crow's nest. From here the lookout had spotted the iceberg seconds before it hit the ship. We looked near the bow for the hole made by the iceberg. But it was covered with mud.

I wondered what might lie on the ocean floor between the two parts of the wreck. When the *Titanic* broke in two, thousands of objects fell out. We found many of them still lying where they had fallen. It was like visiting a huge underwater museum.

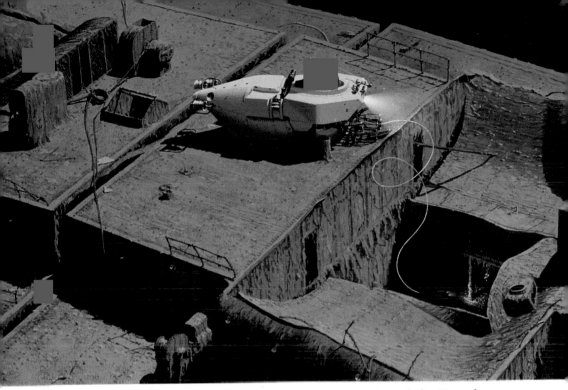

Alvin waits while *JJ* explores the ruined Grand Staircase.

The Grand Staircase in 1912.

Today coral sprouts from one of the remaining light fixtures near the staircase.

A rust-covered bathtub.

The side of one of
the benches from the
ship's deck.

The handle of the *Titanic's*
safe was still shiny.

There were pots and pans, cups and saucers, boots, bathtubs, suitcases, and even a safe with a shiny brass handle.

Before we left the *Titanic* we placed two metal plaques on its decks. The one on the stern section is in memory of all the passengers who lost their lives. The plaque on the bow section asks anyone else who visits the *Titanic* to leave it in peace.

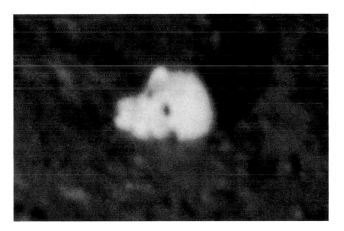

This china head is all that remains of what was once an expensive doll.

Ken Marshall '87 ©

Epilogue

I was sorry when our trips to the *Titanic* were finished. But I was proud of what we had done. We found the ship. And we took many beautiful pictures of it. People all over the world would be able to "visit" the wreck when they saw *JJ*'s pictures. They would think about the people who had sailed on the *Titanic* — those who had lost their lives as well as the survivors.

Ruth Becker and her family had been lucky. Ruth grew up to become a teacher. She married and had three children. Like many *Titanic* survivors, Ruth wouldn't talk about the sinking. Her children didn't even know she had been on the ship.

JJ takes a close-up look at one of the *Titanic*'s anchors.

She finally began to talk about her experience toward the end of her life. When she was eighty-five years old, Ruth saw pictures of the wreck on the ocean floor. When Ruth was ninety, she went on her first sea voyage since the *Titanic*. She died later that year.

After our trip, another group of people went down to the *Titanic*. They brought up many things from the wreck — the ship's telephone and the bell from the crow's nest, some china, a leather bag full of jewelry and money, and hundreds of other objects.

I was very sad when I heard this. The *Titanic* should be left in peace as a monument to those who lost their lives on that cold, starry night so long ago.